NEVER KNEW WHAT'S WRIGHT

A COLLECTION OF POEMS AND QUOTES

PIYUSH YADAV

Copyright © Piyush Yadav
All Rights Reserved.

This book has been published with all efforts taken to make the material error-free after the consent of the author. However, the author and the publisher do not assume and hereby disclaim any liability to any party for any loss, damage, or disruption caused by errors or omissions, whether such errors or omissions result from negligence, accident, or any other cause.

While every effort has been made to avoid any mistake or omission, this publication is being sold on the condition and understanding that neither the author nor the publishers or printers would be liable in any manner to any person by reason of any mistake or omission in this publication or for any action taken or omitted to be taken or advice rendered or accepted on the basis of this work. For any defect in printing or binding the publishers will be liable only to replace the defective copy by another copy of this work then available.

Contents

Poems

1. Wish

Wish the sunrises at night,
To unravel what's inside of us
To show what's and what is not,
To give peace of bitter hope.
Wish the moon lights us in the daytime,
To be a perfect blend of present and rewind,
To colour the crimson white again,
To take us back to where we have been.
Wish the summer feels cold again,
To hide the pain long forgotten,
To kiss the sun on the forehead,
To be blind the lights for the skin.
Wishes take you far away,
Only to take you back forward again,
Only to lie for a man,
Only to drown in a foreign land.

Wishes are not hopes,
To fulfil imagination,
To contentment ever far-reaching,
To start over again.

2. Tangent

Tangent took you, took me,
An undefined creature, the curse,
Life of a pig, death of a dog,
Do you understand what I'm saying?
Tangent looks at you, looks at me,
An unfinished business, a tribulation,
Takes you far from here, to somewhere here near,
Do you see where I'm going?
Tangent hears you, hears me,
An unopened present, an unfurled past,
Take a deep suspire, in the underwater empire,
Do you how it feels?
Tangent, one and two, two and one,
Died down with life, alive in its death,
A promise of deception, an uncomplicated contradiction,
Do hear my heartbeats?
Look at you, Look at me,
Hear me not, hear you soon,
Pick it up, put it down,
Do you know what it's like?
Do you know what it's about?
Or are you just a tangent?

3. Haven't you heard?

Haven't you heard?
The stars are falling from the sky,
Burning willfully, you can hear them cry.
Unforgettables are now a part of your reminiscences,
When breathe gently touching the tender skin was not enough,
we now made peace with those long distances.
Haven't you heard?
The arms stretching toward the sky are now wearily lying on the
cold ground,
What used to be so neighbouring, is now nowhere to be found.
In dread, do we live, keep on living and die?
Do birds with broken wings ever fly?

4. Alive

No motion, no speed, am I even alive anymore?
No emotion, no heed, have I lost that significant core?
Worried about the things that don't even exist;
Obtusely walking through this never-ending mist.
I won't lie I'm scared to death that I'll never be afraid;
Nightmares become fairs and dreadful thoughts, just another
black parade.
I've lost I more times than I can count;
I always run into this melancholy to mount.
Always come back to these hidden unhealed scars, yes they were
deep;
A reminder, a reminisce and memories that I've to keep.
Is this a strayed call for succour, maybe?
Or am I just a midget crybaby?
I don't know how to put feelings in words,
But I want to feel alive like those infinitely flying birds.
If I can breathe, feel, and express, and it's not a jest;
I'd feel alive again or get a perpetual rest.
Animate me or burn me, just set me free,
Touch me, hold me or cut me like a tree.
But

If I can breathe the lost air again, I wouldn't resist wheezing and
let the whole world know,
I'm still here, bright, shiny and always ready to go.

5. Perhaps

Perhaps,
We think a lot, try to sort,
the life which we all have.
Close your eyes, otherwise,
Movement is all we have.
Saw the black; saw the white; Is it a battle or just another street
fight?
Now perspective is all we have.
Perhaps,
if we stand still or climb the tallest hill,
the circle is all we have.
So stand up or climb down, laugh or simply frown,
This moment is all we have.
Perhaps,
if we had time, mind with less grime,
introspection is all we have.
But until then, I'm in my den, so blue and no clue
Of what I have.

6. Beyond

The only sky we ever knew,
is filled with dark clouds now.
"What is what?" and "what is that?",
even the answer comes with a how.
So, we refocused our view and saw the alluring greenfield;
Oh so lovely, and the beauty they yield.
But the dark clouds may destroy them, yes they may.
If you don't understand it,
there's more heed that you need to pay....

7. Education Dis-System

As a dense child, I had profound dreams,
To Slit the sky of prospects and reach new extremes.
But alas, now I feel shame for my futile existence,
Cause my magnificent feathers have been chopped off by our
rotten education dis-system.
As a gullible guy, I saw magic in everything in my early teens,
To explore the unknown and see all the corners and smithereens.
But no, crushed between the four walls of resistance,
Struck between the narrow lines and this fettered education dis-
system.
As a man's consequence, I've earned the empty dimes and walked
meaningless scenes,
To still hope and not let the world turn me into a mindless
machine.
But look, I've found myself struck in this looping ecosystem,
I'm suffocating, breathless and slowly dying thanks to this lovely
education dis-system.
I guess I still am a dreamer and yet I believe,
I believe in change and one day this world will get a soft relief.
Until it does, I will still be mad, will still be persistent,
To liberate minds, to liberate souls and to learn and teach
beyond this education system.

8. Her Name

Met her last dubious morning to know her peculiar name;
she put velvety fingers on my rocky lips, it was only the start of
the game.
My dry lips, thirsty for answers can't bear it anymore;
Looking for unsolved puzzles, knocking on every fastened door.
Met her last inky afternoon to talk about fatuous life;
Endless thought and fractious plight.
More confusion and itchy discomfort;
yet can see some losing triumphant.
Met her in the puzzled evening, she held me close,
I cried tears of relief and felt the combobulating wind blows.
After such a massive loss, everything seems strangely nice,
To gain something, one has to pay a hefty price.
Met her at dazzling night, she stood a little far,
she screams the joyous words, " I hope you now know the name
and who we are"
Light flashes, doubts turn into ashes and I realise;
The truth of who we are, no separated, but one and only one,
with never-ending size.
Didn't meet her the next neo morning, I smiled as wide as I can,
she has always been a part of me and this indisputable plan.

9. A Bird's Dream

As the days pass by,
the bird remembers jiffy in which she used to fly.
Slowly dread seems to take over her little bird heart,
all the valleys she conquered are now destroyed by this empty
rampart.
Now, in insomniac nightmares, hear her pitiful scream,
wait and dream little bird, dream.

As the days pass by,
the bird feels the old dying night sigh.
Slowly despondency seems to take over her little bird spirit,
all the laughing comrades she used to adore are now preterite.
Now, in forlorn nightmares, see her sadden gleam,
hold on, dream little bird dream.

As the days pass by,
the bird waves the outside world goodbye.
Slowly recollecting the memories of old cage life,
all the lesson she learned but this time, the feathers can't carry
her to Fife.
As the days pass by,
the bird looks at the blue shiny sky.

Slowly feeling the heavy breeze,
all the dread it made her feel, now putting her at ease.
Now, in nightmare, feel what she can redeem,
a little longer, dream little bird dream.

As the days pass by,
the bird realises the bright shining sunrise.
Slowly comprehending what the things she wishes for,
all the nameless freedom and much much more.
Now, nightmares are over, see what's supreme,
it's almost time, dream little bird dream.
Closed eyes, she sees the alluring blue; straight face, her grin
brighter than the moon; and ears to hear the air-cutting stream,
Wish and hope, her eyes will fulfill the last sweet fictitious
dream.

10. Liberate

Broken glasses of self show more reflection of you,
empty walls cage the shattered distorted hue.
Yet if you survive the jungle of life, you'll have your chance,
to show the dull world your moonlight dance.
And liberate
Don't expect to see the face of truth if you keep throwing the
pebbles of lies,
It's the pond of regrets, it fills with your tears of shame before it
dries.
Yet if you can see yourself with your eyelids closed, you'll have
your hope,
to see this black and white world with beautiful colours of a
kaleidoscope.
And liberate
All hard waxes of tall candles, we fear melting away,
Melting, drying, forming, why can't we reckon the price of barter
that we have to pay?
Yet, if you can accept the unrecognisable "I", you'll have your
insight,
and no power can stop your ceaseless will to fight.
And liberate.

11. Seeking me

Take a look in your eyes,
Tell me what do you see?
As many people on Earth, as there can be!
Yet, none in this crowd can find "He".
This "he" he is looking for, is me.
Why in this crowd, consist of oh so many,
his worth is less than tiny worthless a penny.
The lesser you look, the more you see.
Only dread, fear, agony and no point to plea.
Don't look in the crowd, but look at it, if hope is what you wish
to find.
Me in you and you in me, espy if you are not yet blind!

12. Waiting

Waiting for the clouds to fade;
I'm mostly done with this charade.
How long do I have to wait for it to shine?
There are times I don't see a single silver line.
Waiting for the disaster of my deed;
I'm mostly tired to plead.
How long do I have to wait for the thunder to strike?
There are times I see the mirror and there's nothing to like.
Waiting for the world to change;
I'm mostly lost in what's normally called strange.
How long do I have to pretend I don't care?
There are times when it seems the fight ain't fair.
Waiting for a moment to lose it all;
I'm mostly surrounded by these empty walls.
How long do I have to be who I'm not?
There are times I wish to execute my own plot.
Waiting for the feelings to come back;
I'm mostly grey, a mixture of white and black.
How long do I have to wait for these colours to vanish?
There are times I wish to see my hand with a blemish.
Waiting for the bed of roses to lay forever;
I'm mostly interested in not waking up ever.

How long do I have to wear these scars that look like a smile?
There are times I wish to end this guile.
Waiting makes one old,
Waiting creates many stories to be told.
No matter how many things I've to wait for;
I'm waiting to be missed when I'm late.

Quotes

13. Hope

"Hope brings despair unless you become one."

"Hoping is far less disappointing than wishing, it gives one a sense of responsibility."

"Hope comes to those who have faith; Faith comes to those who have will; Will is an attitude of the brave; And brave are those you have lived not survived."

"A promise made to self brings a lot of hope in oneself; choose your words wisely when you talk to yourself."

"I think therefore I'm and perhaps I hope therefore everything else is."

"To be broken is accidental, to pick up the broken pieces of self and start over again is a choice. These broken pieces can be glued back with an adhesive called hope."

"Trust is built upon hope for things to be all right."

"Hope, contrary to popular understanding, is a virtue of strong."

"If you can breathe, the existence has yet not given up on you."

14. Faith

"What is not understood but trusted is faith."
"When I believe things will get better eventually, they do. If I don't, they might never."
"Weight of the world can crush you down, give some of it to faith."
"Fears fought with faith wins."
"Faith: soothes the mind, fuels the soul."
"I closed my eyes, there was nothing but my faith that there is."
"Faith doesn't mean following blindly, but choosing to do so based on 100s of experiences."
"Don't test your faith, but experience it. Something does make sense no matter how hard we try to make a sense out of it."
"I'm nothing but a manifestation of your faith and trust in existence."

15. Beauty

"All colours look so bright in black, do they not?"

"If I would kiss your cheeks, it'd be to see those blushes. You look so beautiful when you put them on."

"Heaven is nothing but a manifestation of man's pursuit for beauty."

"I saw, I felt and I fell. That's the power of beauty."
"Beautifulness and ugliness have one similarity, both require dark to confirm their existence."

"Beauty is a medicine for the broken."

"Beauty is the life force that keeps the world kind if you think about it."

16. End

"Everything end, good and bad, happy and sad, intellect and mad. So, don't frown or smile all the time."

"Without an end, there's no point in living."

"End is the most dreadful sense of satisfaction we all strive eventually without realising it."

"A sense of understanding of what end makes one humble, grounded and goal-oriented."

"To live in luxury is to die in poverty."

"An ending followed by credits brings new beginnings."

"Nothing brings results better than an end."

"There is a possibility that is nothing like an absolute end. So, until we meet again."